The Day
The Towers Fell
The Story of September 11, 2001

by Maureen Crethan Santora

ILLUSTRATED BY PATRICIA SANTORA CARDONA

This book is dedicated to all the mommies, daddies, sons, daughters, aunts, uncles, brothers, sisters, cousins, grandparents, nephews, nieces and friends who died on September 11, 2001, THE DAY THE TOWERS FELL.

It is especially dedicated to Firefighter Christopher A. Santora my son who with 342 of his fellow firefighters died on that fateful day. May they always be remembered and may they rest in peace. May all of us who remain never forget that horrible day. May the memories of our loved ones be with us forever.

Maureen Santora

The sun shone brightly as mommies and daddies and sons and daughters and grandparents and aunts and uncles and brothers and sisters and cousins and nieces and nephews and friends went to work.

Some people rode subway trains and buses and cars. Some people walked or roller-skated or biked.

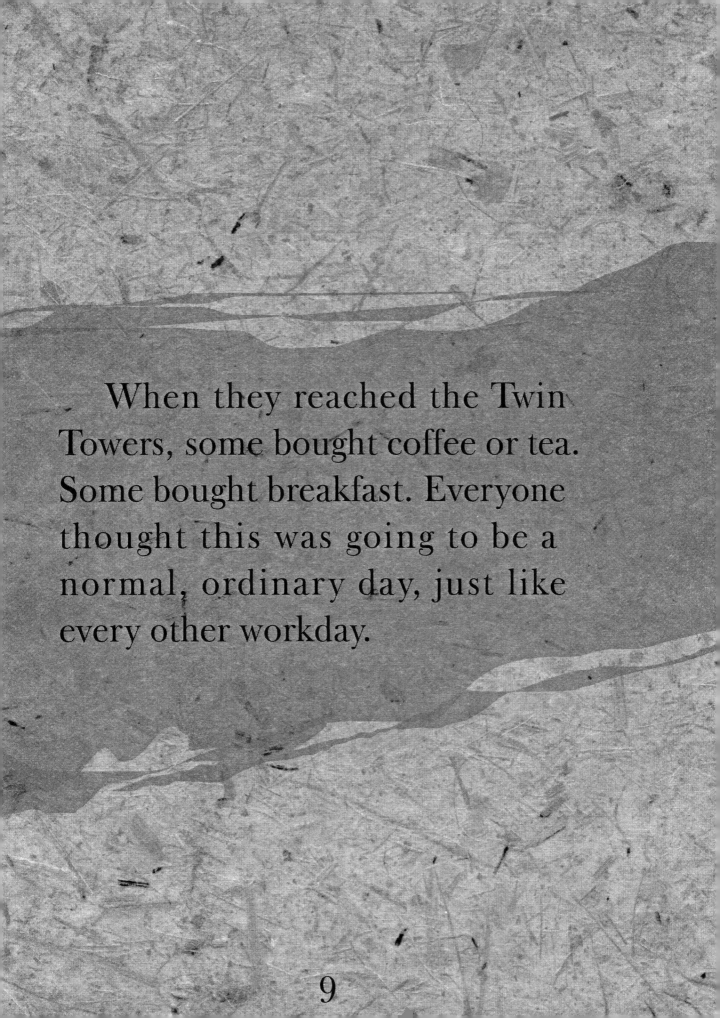

When they reached the Twin Towers, some bought coffee or tea. Some bought breakfast. Everyone thought this was going to be a normal, ordinary day, just like every other workday.

In the fire houses some firemen were getting to work for the morning tour. Others were getting ready to go home after working all night. They were going home to their families.

Then something terrible happened. A plane flew into one of the Twin Towers. Tower One had been hit. Flames and dark thick smoke came out of the building. Many people thought it was an accident. No one could imagine that a plane would deliberately fly into one of the tallest buildings in the world.

Some people were told to stay calm and go back to work. Others started to walk down the many steps to get out. People were afraid but most did not think this was an act of terror or hatred.

15

Firefighters were called to the scene. Police and Emergency workers rushed to help. Ambulances drove to the site. Doctors and nurses went to help the injured.

Then the unthinkable occurred. The second Twin Tower was hit by another plane. This time, everyone knew that this was not an accident. People were afraid and scared. They panicked! They knew their lives were in danger.

19

Firefighters were sent into the buildings to help people get out. They were sent in to try to put out the fires. Everyone began to rush out of the buildings. No one thought the Twin Towers were going to collapse. Everyone hoped that they would get out.

Firefighters were still walking up the stairs helping people to get out of the buildings. They walked with all their gear on. They helped people who were hurt.

All of a sudden Tower Two collapsed. Many people and firefighters were trapped inside. There was smoke and dust and debris. People who had gotten out of the buildings began to run and scream. There was chaos. All of the News stations on T.V. and the radio spoke about the terrible event.

Then Tower One collapsed. As the world watched in horror everyone knew that mommies and daddies and sons and daughters and grandparents and aunts and uncles and brothers and sisters and cousins and nieces and nephews and friends were still inside. So were the Firefighters and Police officers and the Emergency Medical Workers who were working to help people.

As the world watched in horror and silence, no one could understand how or why this terrible event had happened. Everyone was in shock. Why would anyone want to kill innocent people? It was an act of hate. How could anyone hate that much?

All of the families and friends of all of the people who died on September 11, 2001 will never be the same. The world will never be the same. Hatred is a terrible thing. It causes pain and suffering and grief.

On September 11, 2001 **The Day the Towers Fell** all of the people of the world saw the effects of hatred. May we always remember what hatred looks like and may we never forget those who died on that terrible day.

FACTS ABOUT SEPTEMBER 11, 2001

The Twin Towers were 2 of 7 buildings on a 16 acre site which made up the World Trade Center.

On September 11, 2001 at 8:46 A.M. the North Tower was hit. At 9:03 A.M. the South Tower was hit. Both buildings were hit by airplanes that left Boston, Massachusetts and were going to Los Angeles, California. The planes were hijacked by terrorists. At 9:59 A.M. the South Tower fell. At 10: 28 A.M. the North Tower fell.

It was the first day of school in New York City. Because of this not all of the people who worked at the World Trade Center were at work. Many were late because they were bringing their children to school.

It is believed that between 25,000 and 30,000 people were rescued by firefighters, police officers and port authority police.

2,750 people died at the World Trade Center. Among them, 343 firefighters died, 23 police officers died and 37 port authority police died.

Many people who lived in the area had to walk over bridges, take ferries either to New Jersey, Brooklyn or Staten Island to escape to safety.

The towers came down straight in a "pancake" fashion. The fires burned for 6 months at the site. Rescue workers worked from September 12, 2001 to May 30, 2002. Many are now very ill because of the toxic air. Residents who lived in the area were not allowed into their homes for many months.

People from all over the world came to help with the rescue. The world mourned the many people who died on September 11, 2001.